Pursued

Understanding and Responding to the Savior Who Pursues

Ginny Fowler

DEDICATION

To Donna McClintock, who has shown us at
Lionheart Children's Academy how important it is to pursue Jesus.
You have left an indelible mark with your love for Christ, heart for
worship, listening ears, and bold leadership. Your legacy is servant-
leaders pursuing Christ and pursuing His desire for us to make an
eternal impact on lives big and small.

CONTENTS

DAY 1 – A SEAT AT THE TABLE

Now the tax collectors and sinners were all gathering around to hear Jesus. But the Pharisees and the teachers of the law muttered, "This man welcomes sinners and eats with them." (Luke 15:1-2)

Imagine your middle school lunchroom. There are tables that feel reserved and exclusive. Tables that are empty. Tables you eye and want to sit at. Maybe there's ease and comfort, or maybe you are like me in this memory, and it takes some courage to pull up a seat at any table.

Before we come to the parables in Luke 15, we see Jesus rearranging the table rules: strict rules about who could eat with whom, and where they could sit. This doesn't feel like a big deal to us, but the table was a prized place and spoke to high status, honor, spiritual purity, and righteous belonging. If Jesus included someone at His table, He was including them in His Kingdom. All they had to do was respond to His message. They didn't have to earn it or clean themselves up. They just had to listen and respond with a yes to Him.

The tax collectors and "sinners," categorized by others as traitors and outcasts, had listened to Jesus. They realized they needed forgiveness, and responded to His good news and call to repent. Jesus sat at their table, inviting them into His Kingdom. This caused a problem with the Pharisees.

The Pharisees felt they had worked really hard to keep God's law and in turn, keep God's favor. They felt if they were extra good, God would be good to them and His Kingdom would be theirs. They were frustrated by the rule breakers and how Jesus was pursuing them, inviting them to follow Him, and even eating with them.

It's to these groups He tells three parables of wandering, losing, finding, restoring, and celebrating. Each listener was going to take something just a little bit different from the stories.

Who do you identify with in this story? The tax collectors and "sinners"? The Pharisees? A mix? Why?

Did you know that Jesus had room at His table for both? He wanted everyone to listen, see their real standing as sinners in need of a Savior, and turn to Him. Responding to Him with a yes, a chair of honor would slide out and gracious friends would make room for one more, as though they'd just been waiting for that one to come and sit down and be with Jesus.

There's a seat at His table for you. Will you listen and respond? Will you release trying to earn His love and favor? Will you stop trying to cover yourself and clean yourself up first? Will you stop treating a King like karma? Will you receive good news and say yes? Will you turn away from sin and striving and turn to Him? There's a seat waiting for you.

Jesus, I find myself in that crowd. You are speaking to me. May I have ears to hear and respond. I lay down my pride, my defenses, my old attitudes and habits, and I come to you. Thank You that because of Your life, death, and resurrection, I have new life! You replace my shame with honor, my mess with purity, and my cast-down soul with Your righteousness. Thank You, my King, that I have been invited into Your Kingdom. Thank you that there has always been a seat at Your table for me. In Jesus' Name, Amen

DAY 2 - DESIRE

Then Jesus told them this parable: "Suppose one of you has a hundred sheep and loses one of them. Doesn't he leave the ninety-nine in the open country and go after the lost sheep until he finds it? (Luke 15:3-4)

Like children, let's ask questions. There are one hundred sheep, and the shepherd loses one. Where did it go? Why did it leave? What was this sheep pursuing that it wandered from the shepherd?

Sheep follow their noses and what they want to eat. Sheep follow their desires. At first, this can be just an innocent thing. Desire can be a good thing. God gave us *desire* all the way back in the Garden. For Adam and Eve, any desires or wants they had spiritually, emotionally, or physically could be met in God, one another, or their environment. Desire wasn't wrong.

We are told in scripture that we can have good desires that come from God and can be included in His ways and ours. But any desire can take a turn. Where do good desires turn to things that lead us away from the shepherd?

Desires gone wrong are all about us: satisfying or fulfilling ourselves, going our own way to get what we want so we can have something, feel something, or be something. We fill ourselves with what we see as best. We will ultimately desire our good without our God.

When we have desire, if we go anywhere other than God to meet it, our desires will take a turn, entice us to sin, and draw us away-away-away from God.

Here's a list of common heart cravings, or desires.
- worthy, acceptable
- desired/desirable
- secure (in a relationship, financially, in my job, etc.)
- in control
- needed
- wanted, connected to someone
- valued, prioritized
- recognized, not taken for granted
- right, vindicated
- righteous, "okay"
- successful, accomplished, intelligent
- liked
- comfortable. rested
- respected
- beautiful, attractive
- approved of (by spouse, supervisor, neighbors, or ____)[i]

3

A way to figure out if you have a desire that's taking a turn is to ask: What am I striving for, fighting for, defending, prioritizing over almost everything, afraid of, consistently thinking about and arranging my life around? Who/where am I looking to get this need/want met?

I know I have a desire to be wanted and loved. If I serve others to be needed, or in hopes that I will be thanked and appreciated, then my desire has taken a turn and is enticing me to sin with selfish motives and pride. It's not a bad desire to be wanted and loved. And it's not bad to serve others, or even be appreciated. But what my heart truly desires and how I am looking to satisfy this desire are what matters.

Today, take a moment with this list and with Jesus. Consider if any of your needs or desires are taking a turn and drawing you away from Jesus. Are you trying to satisfy yourself, go your own way to get what you want so you can have something, feel something, or be something? What's your real need?

If I only had_____ then I'd be/feel _(desire, need hope, want)_.

OR

I am looking for _____ to meet my need/desire for _____.

Thank you, Lord, that I can be honest with You. You already know what's in my heart and my thoughts (Ps. 139:1-4). Lord, help me to see what I truly desire and want, and how I am pursuing that desire. I trust that Your light on this is to help me heal and bring me back toward You. In Jesus' Name, Amen.

DAY 3 - DISTRACTED

We must pay more careful attention, therefore, to what we have heard,
so that we do not drift away. (Hebrews 2:1)

Did you know that "people receive between 60 and 80 daily
notifications on average, and some of us may get as many as 200?"[ii]
Researchers are finding that notifications that pop up, buzz, or ding are
interrupting and even rewiring how our brains focus. We are mentally
scattered--distracted and disrupted by alerts, notifications, and haptics.

Being focused, or anchored, is critical to our brains in decision-making,
relationships, and life in general. It's important in our spiritual lives too.

If it's not desire-gone-wrong, it's distraction that can lead us from our
Shepherd. We get busy, we stop listening to the Father through His
word thinking we'll do it tomorrow, we slowly separate from other
followers of Jesus, we numb instead of rest and reconnect with God, we
start to rely on our own strength and our own ways of figuring things out.
We start to drift away from God with a series of small self-sufficient
decisions or a series of subtle shrugs...and we look up and realize we are
far from the Shepherd and don't know how we got here, or how our lives
look the way they look. We got distracted and we've somehow drifted.

Hebrews tells us that drifting is like a boat that passively floats by the
docking point in the harbor. It's taken along by the current and pushed
away from safety, security, and provision. To drift doesn't take any effort
at all. It just happens all on its own. Drifting is always unintentional. No
one ever means to drift.

Sailing to the harbor and the secure point takes intentionality. Our verse
tells us we need to pay more careful attention to what we have heard.
We need to intentionally listen to the truth, really carefully consider it
and think it over, meditate on what it means for our lives, and respond.
This active pursuit of God and His word will keep us from distractions
and drifting. It will draw us to the Shepherd and His security and
provision.

List here any things that might be distracting you from Jesus, and
interrupting your focus on Him. Talk to God about drifting and listen for

His way for you to intentionally pursue Him and His word.

*Lord, life with You is active and intentional. It takes effort to fight the distractions of life and not drift. It's a battle because the enemy knows what happens in heaven and on earth when Your people truly pursue and follow You—when **I** pursue and follow You. Lord, I need Your "want to" to want to pursue You. You are the God of my heart and know my desires. And You can affect my desire to pursue You if I will open that to You. So I do. Here I am, Lord. I want to follow You. In Jesus' Name, Amen.*

DAY 4 - HE PURSUES US

Then Jesus told them this parable: "Suppose one of you has a hundred sheep and loses one of them. Doesn't he leave the ninety-nine in the open country and go after the lost sheep until he finds it? And when he finds it, he joyfully puts it on his shoulders and goes home.
(Luke 15:3-6a)

Distracted or pursuing how we can meet our own desires and needs—when we are not pursuing Jesus—He pursues us. He leaves the 99 (safely, by the way) because the one sheep matter. He is relentless. He retraces the steps of our wandering with His gracious feet to come after us.

Why does He pursue us?

It's what He came to do. "For the Son of Man came to seek and to save the lost" (Lk. 19:10). Even when we lost our way and didn't mean to. Even when we didn't understand our own heart cravings and where pursuing them apart from Him would take us. Even when we intentionally set out on our own. It's why He came to us. And so He comes after us.

We belong to Him. He carries the sheep *home*. That means it belongs to Him. "It is He who made us, and we are His; we are His people, the sheep of His pasture" (Ps. 100:3) "I am the Good Shepherd. The Good Shepherd lays down His life for the sheep...I know my sheep and My sheep know Me" (Jn. 10:11,14). Bad shepherds and hired hands don't personally care about sheep because they don't belong to them. But Jesus deeply cares for those who are His. He will pursue us with goodness and lovingkindness because we belong to Him. We see this more as we look at Psalm 23 together.

It's for His name's sake. Because He's the Good Shepherd and we belong to Him, it would tarnish His name, reputation, and integrity if He left us out there where our distractions and desires had taken us. He acts to protect us and to protect His name and uphold His holiness and goodness.

He knows that His sheep are prone to follow their own desires and distractions. And so He pursues us.

Briefly share a time when Jesus pursued you (or maybe He's pursuing you right now). Highlight Him, how He pursued you, and how you knew it was Him.

Thank You, Good Shepherd, that You came to seek and save me. Thank You that I belong to You and I am never too far gone for You to come after me and find me. Thank You that You act out of goodness and lovingkindness. Thank You for pursuing me. In Jesus' Name, Amen.

DAY 5 - IN HIS ARMS

He tends His flock like a shepherd: He gathers the lambs in His arms and carries them close to His heart; He gently leads those that have young. (Isaiah 40:11)

And when he finds it, he joyfully puts it on his shoulders and goes home. Then he calls his friends and neighbors together and says, 'Rejoice with me; I have found my lost sheep.' I tell you that in the same way there will be more rejoicing in heaven over one sinner who repents than over ninety-nine righteous persons who do not need to repent. (Luke 15:5-7)

When we wander and when we sin, many of us think that God is mad at us - angry eyebrows and keeping us at arm's length, or just letting us go to hurt ourselves, or worse. And I think we think that because truthfully that's what our wandering and sin deserve. But our Savior pursues us so that He can take us in His arms and joyfully carry us home.

Psalm 51:1 says it's out of His unfailing love, even when we've failed, and out of His great compassion, even when we drifted and wandered or intentionally set out to meet our needs apart from Him—that He forgives us and brings us back. Unfailing love and great compassion are the two arms underneath us, as He carries us close to His heart.

On the journey home on the Shepherd's shoulders, the sheep's head would rest close and hear the Shepherd's heart. The sheep would retread with the Savior the path that it had wandered on, not with shame, but with perspective, not close to the dirt, but with His view from His shoulders. When we see our sin and wandering from His perspective and hear His heart, then we can understand it, process it, and leave it behind. Then we can move forward with Him.

Jesus' unfailing love, great compassion, gentle and humble heart, and truthful perspective will carry you back to where you were meant to be— close to Him, following Him on His paths, leaving behind the old story.

What's speaking to you today? His arms of love and compassion? His gentle and humble heartbeat? His perspective on the path that led you astray? His grace that defeats shame and rejoices over His redemption? Lean on Jesus today and listen. That will be your prayer: *lean and listen.*

DAY 6 – THE ULTIMATE NEED-MEETER

I am the LORD your God, Who brought you up out of Egypt. Open wide your mouth and I will fill it. (Psalm 81:11)

*Bless and affectionately praise the Lord, O my soul, And all that is [deep] within me, bless His holy name. Bless and affectionately praise the Lord, O my soul, And do not forget any of His benefits; Who forgives all your sins, Who heals all your diseases; Who redeems your life from the pit, Who crowns you [lavishly] with lovingkindness and tender mercy; **Who satisfies your years [desires] with good things**, So that your youth is renewed like the [soaring] eagle.*
(Psalm 103:1-5, AMP)

If you go back to page 3 and look at the list of heart cravings, each one of those is one Jesus can meet. We may feel a slight snag in our hearts here, wondering if that's really true, if His answer will really be good enough, or if that's just hyper-spiritual but not really practical.

Here are two things I have learned: the enemy's game from the Garden was to get us to question God's goodness and if He was holding out on us when in truth He had our best and provided it if we would go to Him. Second, Jesus always did things that were highly practical **and** deeply spiritual. Think about His miracles. Healing, feeding, **and** spiritually transforming. He is ready to truly satisfy our needs and desires if we will bring them to Him and examine them with Him.

Take my desire to be wanted and loved. I need someone or something that can fully handle the vastness and weight of my need. People, even good ones, may fail to recognize me, appreciate me, or ask me for help or counsel. Applause fades. And even the best love on earth can still be marred by the fact that we are broken people. So where can I go to truly have my desire met? I can keep on trying with people or accomplishments. I can strive, or love to be loved. Or I can open myself up to Jesus.

I know I am wanted, because even if I were the only person on earth, Jesus would have come—just for me. I hear Him whisper my name every morning asking me to come and spend time with Him. I know I am loved completely and fully because the Bible overflows with truths about God's lavish love for me. Because Jesus came and because He delights to love me, I know that I am wanted and beloved. This has been practical for me because I can stand firm in a new place with new people and know I am wanted. I can serve and love others without needing accolades because Jesus loves and wants me for me—not for what I do.

Let's quickly do one more. I want to be in control. We all do! It provides a feeling of safety and security and knowing what's coming so I can handle it well for myself and others. How does control end up looking in our lives? How does it affect our relationships? Do we actually get what we desire?

What if we laid our heads on the Shepherd's chest and heard His heart on control? His faithful word is that we are not in control because we are human. But, He is. He can see everything and knows everything. He holds our lives together and is closer to us than our own breath. We get to rely on the One Who is in control of all things. So He won't meet our desire to be in control, but He will satisfy the deeper longing to be held together and secure.

"I have set the Lord continually before me; Because He is at my right hand, I will not be shaken. Therefore my heart is glad and my glory [my innermost self] rejoices; My body too will dwell [confidently] in safety [and security]" (Ps. 16:8-9). As we fix our eyes on Him, we will readily identify His presence and care, and true security will come without the negative effects of attempting control.

He will fully satisfy our desires or He will identify the deeper root of our desires and reframe them so He can meet what we actually need. His response will be deeply spiritual and highly practical.

Sit with your desires and needs. Open up the part of you that is hungry and ask the One who brought you out of sin and being held captive by things that were never meant to master you—ask Him to show you your real desires and needs. Ask Him how He wants to fill and satisfy you or give you something even better. Write or draw your own prayer here.

Now it's your turn. Take a desire or need you have and ask God to show you how He fills and satisfies it.

Since I have Jesus, I am _____ or I can feel/be _____.

Because Jesus has done/given _____ I am/can feel_____.

God's word promises me _____ so I am/ can be/ feel _____.

If you don't have an answer yet, that's OK! Keep opening up to Jesus. Stay in His word. He'll speak and reveal.

DAY 7 - REPENT

I tell you that in the same way there will be more rejoicing in heaven over one sinner who repents than over ninety-nine righteous persons who do not need to repent. (Luke 15:7)

Repent, then, and turn to God, so that your sins may be wiped out, that times of refreshing may come from the Lord. (Acts 3:19)

Did you know that in the Bible, anytime the word *listen* or *hear* is used in connection with the teachings of the Lord, the idea is to listen and respond? Those two things always go together. When Jesus shared the parable of The Lost Sheep, He wasn't just telling an encouraging or convicting story. The listeners had an opportunity to respond.

How do we respond?

We've explored what it means to bring our needs and wants to Jesus, and we'll continue to explore that. Another way is to respond by repenting.

This parable is about grace. It's about the grace that kept the 99 safely where they needed to be and equal grace to go find the one. Grace finds you where you are as you are, but does not leave you where you are as you are. The work of grace in our lives enlightens our eyes to what we need to turn from and turn to Jesus.

To repent is to turn around. Repentance is not a change in your behavior. It's a change in your god that results in a change in your behavior.[iii] Think about the desires that drew us away, and how they got twisted and came to rule us.

We are going to take all that back to God and "God, You know I want/need _____. I have found myself being pulled to meeting my own needs/desires or wanting this apart from You. I have pursued this and allowed it to rule my attitudes, actions, behaviors, and/or thoughts. I confess that to You, I turn to You, and ask You to meet my needs." Turning to God is the beginning of how grace can then take effect and change us from the inside out.

When we repent and turn to God not only are our sins completely erased (incredible!) but our hearts become reoriented and reordered to follow Him. And that's when refreshing comes to us. Doesn't that sound like a cleansing rainstorm that washes away the heat and dust and ushers in that new season you've been waiting for?

We have talked a lot about our desires, and hopefully, you've had a chance to start sorting through them with the Lord. If you haven't already, take time with that prayer above. Turn from the old ways that didn't satisfy you and the things that tried to rule you. Turn to Jesus. The clouds are gathering. Times of refreshing are on their way.

"What you love you will pursue with your life."[iv] Lord, I want to love You and pursue You with my whole life. I can't do that with old stories, old habits, old attitudes, and things that try to rule me that aren't You. I turn away from those and follow after You. You're my Shepherd. You have called me by name and are leading me out (Jn. 10:3b) of old things and into a life under Your care, Your rule, and Your love. As I turn and follow You, You promise me that You will bring refreshing to my life. Thank You, Good Shepherd and Savior. In Jesus' Name, Amen.

DAY 8 - CELEBRATE

And when he finds it, he joyfully puts it on his shoulders and goes home. Then he calls his friends and neighbors together and says, 'Rejoice with me; I have found my lost sheep.' I tell you that in the same way there will be more rejoicing in heaven over one sinner who repents than over ninety-nine righteous persons who do not need to repent. (Luke 15:5-7)

This is how Jesus feels about pursuing and finding us and about our repentance, or returning home! Joy and rejoicing!

The Shepherd hosts a party and invites all His friends and neighbors and says, "Rejoice with **me; I have found my** lost sheep." The original group around Jesus would have been surprised by this. Sure, sheep wander. But as the stories in Luke 15 build, precious coins get lost, and rebellious children make terrible choices and break their parent's hearts. Yet at every turn, finding what was lost is a cause for celebration with the One Who found it.

That last story in Luke 15, the one we know as The Prodigal Son, reveals the hearts of many listeners. What about the son who stayed and obeyed? He did all the right things. But his heart was bitter towards the Father before the prodigal brother ever boldly left to chase his own desires. The son that stayed never went to the Father with his desires and his attitude was that he wasn't a beloved son but rather a slave (v.29). His reaction is supposed to be one of celebrating, but he finds himself refusing to go to the Father. So the Father pursues him too. And pleads with him to celebrate, reminding him he too is beloved, he belongs, and he is blessed. *"My son,' the father said, 'you are always with me, and everything I have is yours. But we had to celebrate and be glad, because this brother of yours was dead and is alive again; he was lost and is found.'"* (Lk. 15:31-32)

The son that had always been good, struggled that the Father let the undeserving come back into His arms. It made more sense to his heart that if you are good, you get favor and blessing. The Pharisees felt this way too. I think sometimes we do too. But if we go back to the concept of grace, God's astounding grace is keeping the 99 sheep and His grace is fully available to the older brother. His grace is pursuing the sheep and beckoning the prodigal son home into His arms. In the end, it's all grace, and the Giver of such grace must be celebrated. "We **had to** celebrate and be glad" (v. 32).

Those who are close to the Shepherd don't resent His grace or get frustrated by the wandering sheep and how He was pursuing it and bringing it home to follow Him. And the Shepherd doesn't get everyone together to tell the story of the shame of the sheep. The same is true for the Father and the wandering son.

No, the focus is not on the sheep, it's on the Shepherd. It's not on the sinner, it's on the Savior.

They celebrate the Shepherd-Father and His heart of love, compassion, and grace. They celebrate His win. They celebrate the honor and integrity of His name and His calling to seek and save the lost.

As beloved children, kept or brought back by grace, we must celebrate the Shepherd anytime there's a story of repentance and coming home, or restoration. It's the surprising heart of God, Who invites us to celebrate instead of sulk, be joyful instead of judge, and remember His Gospel and grace in our own lives too.

Father, sometimes when I try hard to be good, it's because I desire for You to see me and bless me. But it's not because of what I do, but rather what Jesus has done, that I am your beloved child who has been blessed and has full access to You. You see me and are always with me. Thank You for Your grace at work in my own life and Your grace at work in the lives of others. You are worth celebrating, Gracious Father! In Jesus' Name, Amen.

DAY 9 – PURSUING JESUS

Now while they were on their way, Jesus entered a village [called Bethany], and a woman named Martha welcomed Him into her home. She had a sister named Mary, who seated herself at the Lord's feet and was *continually* listening to His teaching. But Martha was very busy *and* distracted with all of her serving responsibilities; and she approached Him and said, "Lord, is it of no concern to You that my sister has left me to do the serving alone? Tell her to help me *and* do her part." But the Lord replied to her, "Martha, Martha, you are worried and bothered *and* anxious about so many things; but *only* one thing is necessary, for Mary has chosen the good part [that which is to her advantage], which will not be taken away from her."
(Luke 10:38-42, AMP)

I think many of us love this story, because we identify with the conflict between sisters, and moreover the conflict inside Martha. She felt torn and worried and bothered and anxious about so many things. Distractions crowded her heart and mind, and she was missing out. I wonder if she knew it, which is why she asked Mary to help so that she too could sit at Jesus' feet, but after she had pursued what she thought was most important.

What Jesus points out to Martha is not that her desire to serve Him is wrong, but that her heart has things in the wrong order. He reframed her desire. He called her to join Mary. Mary had a rightly ordered heart. The one thing that was truly needed was being with Jesus. That was the most important thing. Mary pursued Jesus by sitting at His feet and continually listening, shutting out distractions, and paying attention to Him.

In the Gospels, we find Mary acting like a disciple: sitting at His feet, listening to His teaching, washing His feet by anointing them with oil, and being the first to get to proclaim His resurrection. Her heart pursued Jesus and she didn't just get a lunch with Him, she got lasting truth and a relationship with Him that stayed with her always.

How can we have a rightly ordered heart like Mary? Here are a few ideas on daily pursuing Jesus.

Start each day with Jesus: maybe that's rolling out of bed onto your knees to pray. Maybe that's opening the verse of the day instead of scrolling emails or social media. Maybe that's sitting up and committing the day to Him with gratitude.

Worship Him: Keep our eyes on Him and proclaim Who He is. Sing! Share with friends and co-workers how He has been good.

Listen to His word: Like Mary, sit at His feet. Or like sheep, our heads can still be close to His heart, listening to His heart for us and for others and for His glory through His word.

Wonder: Watching for the good He brings and for how He is at work in our lives and our ministry, and being amazed! Praising Him for it.

Gratitude: Being humble, remembering His far-reaching grace for you and me, and thanking Him for Who He is and what He does.

Taking our needs to Him: I want this... I desire this... God, what do you say? How can You meet this desire?

Talk to Him (and listen!).

Rest with Him: Instead of numbing with things that don't feed your soul and spirit.

Responding to His love by saying yes to walking in His ways: The Bible calls this obeying.

What's our favorite part of daily pursuing Him? What from the list above would you like to engage and enjoy more?

Lord, I can often feel like Martha, especially with the needs around me. Thank You that You didn't shame her but rather reframed her desire. You invite all of us into the most important thing—time and a relationship with You. Thank You that it's lasting and that You promise that if I seek You first, "all these things will be given to me as well" (Matt. 6:33). Show me what it means for me personally to have a rightly ordered heart and pursue You. In Jesus' name, Amen.

DAY 10 – I HAVE EVERYTHING I NEED

The LORD is my shepherd; I have everything I need. (Psalm 23:1, GNT)

For the next several days, we are going to explore what it means to be a sheep under the expert care of the Good Shepherd. Psalm 23 is a very familiar passage. It's a comfort to many. I love parts of scripture that God has written on my heart through experience and even memorization. What I love even more is that His word is alive and active (Heb. 4:12) and God has something in His word every time I come to Him, even in the most familiar passages. Let's pray for fresh eyes and ears as we explore this beloved psalm.

God uses the Shepherd and sheep analogy a lot in scripture. We've already explored some of the verses in John 10, Isaiah 40, and Psalm 100. We see the details most clearly in Psalm 23.

When it says, *The LORD is my Shepherd*, it pairs two names of God together: LORD and Shepherd. LORD is His personal name for His personal people for His personal purposes for His personal glory. It's the name His children can hang on to and believe, knowing He will keep His promises. It's His loving name connected to redemption and restoration.

We get to remember we are led by the Good Shepherd Who relentlessly pursues us with His love, rejoices over us, chose each of us for His purposes out of His sheer delight (Eph. 1:4-6), calls us by name, makes us His own, and delights in caring for us. The Cross has brought us back under His care.

Since we have a Good Shepherd, we have everything we need. Our needs (mental, emotional, spiritual, physical, etc.) are fully met in Him, not in works or people. We are seen and known, and we will never lack the expert care and management of our Shepherd. We'll see in Psalm 23 that we have freedom from fear, tension, aggravation, hunger, and being overwhelmed. We'll see that He guides us to places for our good, even when it's hard, and He prepares the way for us so we can flourish. We have everything we need in our Shepherd.

The question is, do we go to Him? Do we follow Him? Will we believe we lack nothing because we are His?

The LORD is my Shepherd; I have everything I need. Praise Him for being a Good Shepherd, draw close to Him, and tell Him what you need. You can write your prayer here.

DAY 11 - REST

He makes me lie down in green pastures, He leads me beside quiet waters, (Psalm 23:2)

Making a sheep lie down is awkward. They are heavy on top with small legs, and in the animal world, they are seen as easy prey. They feel very vulnerable when they lie down. But shepherds know they need rest.

Making a hard-working, determined, diligent person lay down is awkward. They tend to carry heavier loads than the frames of their souls were made to carry, and it makes them an easy target for overwork, exhaustion, stress, burnout, and unhealthy coping behaviors. They feel vulnerable when they lie down. But the Good Shepherd knows they need rest. So He prepares places and times for them to truly rest.

Some of us are struggling with rest, even though God has provided places for us. It feels awkward and vulnerable. We feel guilty or ineffective if we rest. We feel a fake sense of getting ahead or getting everything done if we cheat on rest. Our lists may be whittled down, but our souls, spirits, and bodies pay the price. We need rest. How can we be intentional in relationships, have a heart to serve, or be tenacious when we are ragged and exhausted?

Before things were broken in the Garden, God gave us a day of rest. He didn't need rest, but He modeled it for us, as a way to pause and look over our lives and see all that God has done. We get to remember that He's the One that really works in us and through us, and so anything good is to His glory. We get to remember we are human and have limits, and trust God with one day where we rest while He keeps our lives and work in His hands. He designed us for work *and* rest.

For sheep to rest, they must have freedom from fear, tension, aggravation, and hunger. They have this because the Shepherd is near. He applies healing with a gentle touch and His presence to the things that bug them and threaten their safety and security. He works to meet their needs. The same is true for us.

God is leading us to places that will support us, comfort us, revive us, give us healthy perspective, and foster our faith if we will look to Him and follow Him. Let Jesus address your fear, tension, aggravations, and hunger. Let Jesus lead you to places and times of rest. It may be awkward and vulnerable at first, but you will find Him there, and in Him, you will find what you need most.

Consider this quote by Elisabeth Elliot, "Rest is a weapon given to us by God. The enemy hates it because He wants us to be stressed and occupied." How could rest be a weapon for you?

Now consider when you will have a chance to rest this week. If you don't see one, ask the Good Shepherd to show you where the green pastures and quiet waters could be in your life, the times and places of rest He can give you. You may have to rearrange some things or say no to things. Pursue Him there and then be with Him there. True rest with Jesus may be one of the most powerful things you experience each week.

DAY 12 - SOUL CARE

He restores my soul. (Psalm 23:3a)

W. Phillip Keller does a masterful job explaining the deeper and practical meaning of this psalm in his book, A Shepherd Looks at Psalm 23. It is here that I learned that sheep follow their desires. They chase after what would taste good to them, so much so that they will eat grass down beyond the roots into the dirty world below the surface. They will gorge themselves to the point where they are bloated and sick, and they will be what's called "cast down." They fall over and without quick intervention, the blood in their body will move to the middle, away from their legs, and they will die from being "cast down."

Shepherds have to keep a close eye on sheep wandering to rich grass and they have to move sheep often, calling them to lift their heads and follow the shepherd away from places that would make them sick if they stayed.

Think about this in a mental and spiritual sense. When we consume too much of something—a conversation we roll around in our heads again and again, bingeing as a way to escape, the approval of others, over-working, gossip about someone, the shame scripts we listen to, or just our own ways or own strength in something. That does something to our soul, or the real, real us deep down. It brings us down and can bring us to a place where we feel gorged, overwhelmed, or like we can't get up and out of that place. We get cast down.

When sheep are cast down they are terrified and frantic. Shepherds go over to them, stand over them, and steady them. They set the sheep upright, and massage the sheep's legs to get the blood going again. This brings the shepherd close to the sheep's ears, so they speak gently and softly to the sheep to reassure it. This brings peace to the sheep until it can move on its own again and follow the shepherd.

When we are cast down, often it is because we have desired too much softness and/or gorged on too much of what's in front of us. He pursues us, picks us up, and holds us upright, using gentle words until we find our feet once again and follow Him.

That's what it means to restore our souls.

Have you consumed too much of something? Are you feeling cast down? Jesus is here. He has you. He is leaning down and speaking gently to you. He is ready to restore your soul.

LORD, thank You for the richness of Your word. Thank You that when I am "cast down" You don't stomp over irritated that I am here again. Instead, Your love for me moves You to pursue me and pick me up. Your peace which passes all understanding is being spoken into my ear. You will stand with me and care for me in this place where I fell until I can walk with You again. You are a Good Shepherd. I trust You to restore my soul. In Jesus' Name, Amen.

DAY 13- PATHWAYS

He guides me in paths of righteousness for His name's sake.
(Psalm 23:3b)

Yesterday, we discovered that shepherds won't let sheep stay somewhere too long because they could get stuck and get sick from it. Shepherds keep sheep moving.

The Good Shepherd guides us on ground or a path that is good for us. He knows what path is best and leads to life and flourishing and which one leads to danger, harm, or death. He won't let us go our own way or follow the whims of our destructive habits. That's a path that would lead our hearts astray.

The Good Shepherd also won't let us stay somewhere until it's unhealthy. He has a plan with right principles to keep us on the move because He knows that's where we'll thrive. So He calls us and leads us out into new places and seasons with Him.

When we are on that path, He is glorified! He guides us on paths of righteousness because it honors Him. People know those sheep are His and He is a Good Shepherd. That's why He will pursue us when we are not pursuing Him. He loves us and wants us on His path for His name's sake.

What kind of path are you on? Are you following the loving voice of the Shepherd to follow Him? Are you walking away towards another path?

Again, our sheep legs can start to carry us away if we question God's goodness on the path of righteousness. He calls us to love others, lay down our pride, use our mouths to build up, honor Him and others with our bodies, tell the truth, be grateful for what we have—and those are just a few things He calls us to that can be challenging on the path of righteousness. But it is for our good that we are on this path.

Write down the good that could come from those areas listed above.

Now imagine the opposite of those things on the list. What are the spiritual, emotional, relational, and physical consequences of that path?

God isn't looking to make life boring or hard. He's looking to bless us, keep us whole, protect us, and have our lives shine back in praise to Him. His path is for our good and His glory.

Jesus, You tell me that following You will not always be easy. I will have to sacrifice, ignore the "wisdom" of the world, and remember Your immense love for me. So I thank You that You are good and You "never deny me my heart's desire unless it's for something better."ⱽ And that better will be found with You on Your path for Your glory. Be my guide. I am ready to follow You. In Jesus' Name, Amen."

DAY 14 – DARK EQUALS NEAR

Even though I walk through the valley of the shadow of death, I will fear no evil, for You are with me... (Psalm 23:4)

You likely know this verse. It's been a huge comfort to many. Let's explore a few subtle truths.

It's personal. If you look at the language in the psalm, David has been calling God "He." Here he switches to "You." David walked through a valley, and he experienced the Lord as his Shepherd, personally close and with him.

Valleys lead to mountains. Shepherds often took sheep through valleys in the late summer to move them from dried-up pastures to mountain tablelands where they could get fresh grass and relief from the heat. But they had to go through the valley to get to the provision the Shepherd had planned on the other side. The Shepherd always went ahead of the sheep to be sure the valley was passable and that the new pasture was ready. He went before the sheep and nothing surprised Him.

They walk through it. Do you see that? We will walk through (not stop or crumble in) dark roads with Jesus. We <u>will</u> make it to the other side.

He is with them. A Shepherd never hurried His sheep but lovingly led the lambs that had never been that way. The older ones had learned to trust Him in the dark, valley places, and so they would follow Him.

Have you ever been on an unknown, unseen, new, or new yet illuminated path with Jesus? We all have been in dark places where the only way was through. The promise is that Jesus is personally with us. He has gone ahead of us and knows the way. There may be things that surprise us, but we know the Shepherd and trust Him. We will make it through. According to this psalm, *dark doesn't equal alone and fear; dark equals near.* The Good Shepherd is with you.

Are you a young sheep or an old one? Are you walking through one of your first valleys or have you followed Jesus through a few valleys before? What has your experience been? Use the space on the next page to share your thoughts.

Seth Condrey's song, "Great Hope, Great God," includes these lyrics:
Lord, when the light isn't here yet
And it's so hard to find where You are
I'll hold on to You while you teach me
to see in the dark

If you are walking through a valley, keep holding on to the Shepherd. If you can't see Him or sense His presence, tell Him that. Many people have experienced dark nights where they cry out, wondering where He is. Keep calling out for Him. Keep putting one foot in front of the other. He is here and He's bringing You through.

Write your prayer to your Shepherd here. He's listening.

DAY 15 – HIDDEN WOUNDS

Your rod and Your staff, they comfort me. (Psalm 23:4c)

Good tools make a huge difference in your work. If you have ever realized you only have a Phillips head screwdriver and you need a flat head, you know what I mean. If you have seen the amazing kitchens, utensils, and machines on cooking shows, you know what a difference tools can make.

When this psalm was written, shepherds had a few main tools that made a difference in their work. They had a rod and a staff.

The rod was for a display of strength, power, and authority to defend the sheep. They didn't use the heavy end on the sheep for any discipline. It was used against the sheep's enemies. From the heavy end, the rod tapered down. The bottom end of the rod was a tool to part the sheep's wool. Sheep would get scratches, cuts, and infections that they couldn't see for themselves. They were hidden wounds that would increase in hurt and truly affect the sheep. These painful spots could only be carefully examined and treated by the shepherd using the rod.

Don't you love God's word? Our Shepherd is our Defender. He fights for us and will come to our aid when our enemies come against us. The Psalms repeat this truth over and over. And, He came to our aid in the ultimate sense by His display of strength, power, and authority over our great foe, Death, when He rose again! Praise God!

He also can see the hidden things in us that are hurting, aching, and festering. He carefully examines us and administers the healing relief we need. He primarily does this through His word. The rod separates wool. It's there that we can finally see what's going on inside, and we can receive the remedy. He also does this through His Spirit. I can say that there have been times that I have encountered the revelation and healing touch of the Shepherd through a conversation with a faithful friend, a worship song, or just quiet prayer with Jesus. Almost all of these still go back to the truth of His word.

"For the word of God is alive and active. Sharper than any double-edged sword, it penetrates even to dividing soul and spirit, joints and marrow; it judges the thoughts and attitudes of the heart. Nothing in all creation is

hidden from God's sight. Everything is uncovered and laid bare before the eyes of him to whom we must give account." (Heb. 4:12-13)

That's a comfort. He sees and knows deeper than we do and He wants to reveal it so He can heal it.

The staff is the Shepherd's tool to draw us to Himself, draw us together, and draw older and younger sheep together. My favorite part of this is that a Shepherd had special sheep he loved. He would use his staff to select that sheep and draw it close to his side so it simply could walk with him and receive his affection. We are all His special sheep. I know your mom said you were her favorite, and she told your sister the same thing. Our infinite God can have infinite favorites. He's drawing you near to love you and walk closely with you.

Today, do you sense God is using the rod or the staff in your life? How is that tool a comfort to you?

Lord, I thank You that You know my hidden hurts and the things about me I can't even see. I thank You that Your word and Your Spirit bring clarity and healing. Thank You that Your staff is all about us walking with You and experiencing Your love for us and our love for each other. Your rod and staff, they comfort me. In Jesus' Name, Amen.

DAY 16 - PURSUING THE ONE WHO HAS GONE AHEAD

You prepare a table before me in the presence of my enemies.
(Psalm 23:5a)

Do you remember when we talked on Day One that you have a seat at the table? This verse can be viewed as a seat at the king's table! David was a shepherd and a king, and he saw God as his shepherd and his King. A king's table was reserved for those whom the king chose. People longed to be invited to that table. David knew he had a seat at The King's table, and a feast with Jesus was ready for him. The same is true for you.

These verses can also interestingly be seen through the eyes of a sheep. The shepherd would lead the sheep through the valley to the table lands or the higher places up in the mountains during the hot season. The shepherd would go ahead of them and root out all the things in the pasture that would hurt the sheep. The shepherd's presence and activity would put the enemy on alert. The shepherd would prepare a tableland ahead of the sheep in the presence of the sheep's enemies.

For us, the Good Shepherd walks our valleys ahead of time. He knows the way through them. The valleys point to the new seasons and to good places He is preparing for us. He has gone ahead of us, coping with the things that would undo us. He has done that in a literal sense as our Savior. Hebrews 2 tells us that He became like us and experienced the deepest struggle with temptation and yet was sinless and victorious (Heb. 2:14-18). He has deep compassion for our sin struggles. He sees our enemies and the things that would tempt us and offers us a way out to victory (1 Cor. 10:13).

He prepares a table for us in the presence of our enemies.

Take a moment and talk to God about something that has been tempting you. He understands, and He already knows.

He wants to hear from you so His presence can cast a glorious shadow over your life and make the enemy flee. He has a way out for you to victory. Ask Him for eyes to see Him and the way out. Then respond. Take the way to victory.

Yes, Good Shepherd, You have gone ahead of me as Savior, and in this journey You have me on with you. Thank You that the enemy is not the "yin" to Your "yang" as though he was an equal to You. He has always been subject to You and by the cross and Your resurrection, he is defeated. He may be able to make things that come against me, but they are not allowed to prosper or come to their full plan (Isa. 54:17). I choose to pursue You and Your way out. I choose to follow You and listen to Your voice. In Jesus' Name, Amen.

DAY 17 – PERFECT PEACE

You anoint my head with oil; my cup overflows. (Psalm 23:5b)

You will keep in perfect peace him whose mind is steadfast because he trusts in You. (Isaiah 26:3)

Look at all that we have learned about who our Good Shepherd is and what He has done, is doing, and will do. What's been the most important thing you have learned about Him so far?

The truths tucked into this psalm have made me love and trust Jesus more.

We have just a few more days in Psalm 23, and the truths about The LORD as our Shepherd are still coming. In verse 5, he talks about anointing his head with oil. Again, this could be seen as royal language as kings were anointed as a part of their crowning.

Sheep can get something called "nasal flies." To spare you the gory details, if you have ever had a gnat go in your nose or eye, you have a small glimpse of this feeling. Now imagine that times 100 but it won't go away. These flies get in a sheep's head and it is so frustrating and aggravating that sheep will go to extreme lengths to try to get the things in their head to stop, including dashing their hard heads on rocks.

Shepherds have a special oil that is like tar that they will pour over a sheep's head to both rid it of the annoying flies and repel the flies in the future. This soothes the sheep and brings it to a place of peace. The shepherd anoints the sheep's head with oil.

What we see in Scripture is that oil often points us to the Holy Spirit. You and I can have nagging thoughts, shame scripts, frustrations, aggravations, and even just petty annoyances. We can feel like those thoughts just swirl around and buzz in our heads and we can't get rid of them.

Our thought lives are more important than we think. They are a common soft spot for the enemy because many of us don't know that he can't read our minds, but he can speak in the spiritual realm, and that's a place where our ears can hear. We'll often wonder where that's coming from or why we can't stop it. Our verses today have our answer.

1. If whatever you are thinking or feeling does not 100% match what God says in His word—stop right there. Pray, starting with yourself, "Lord, whatever part of this thought is from me, I bend my knee to You. I yield to You. Holy Spirit, remind me of the truth (Jn. 14:26)." Then pray, "Whatever is of the darkness, I've yielded my mind to Jesus, so I say no to this thought in Jesus' Name. Leave in Jesus' Name." These aren't magic words or a formula. It's a posture of yielding your mind to the Lord. His authority and the truth of His Spirit will be like oil on your head as you go to the Shepherd to address your thoughts.

2. Let's read Isaiah 26:3 backward to see how God brings peace to our inner world. When we trust in Him, our minds become steadfast instead of swirling, and we experience His peace. The words "perfect peace" are "shalom shalom," which is already peace at 100% with just one shalom. It's like a cup overflowing with God's whole, full peace, or shalom. Are your thoughts ones that focus and trust in God, or are they swirling with lesser things? What parts of your inner world need to yield to or trust God?

3. Finally, a cup that overflows with shalom also overflows with gratitude. Our thought lives and literally, our brains, are transformed by gratitude.

When nagging thoughts, shame scripts, frustrations, aggravations, and even just petty annoyances come, the Holy Spirit is there to calm our swirling inner world and enable us to act and respond as He would. We must trust Him, yield or give all our thoughts to Him, and do so repeatedly since mental gnats will try every day to get inside.

Today, do you have thoughts swirling? Look at #1 and #2 and bring those before the Lord. And, then write down three things you are thankful for that God has provided. Those will be your prayer.

PURSUED

1.

2.

3.

DAY 18 - LOOKING BACK

Surely Your goodness and love will follow me all the days of my life, and I will dwell in the house of the LORD forever. (Psalm 23:6)

Early this summer, my husband and I drove 1000 miles home, bringing a kid and all his belongings back with us. We had to make it all in one drive. That's about 17 hours in the car. When we finally pulled into the driveway, we all breathed out a big sigh.

That drive was a big one, and not just due to the mileage. Our son had been on a journey for a year. There were a lot of valleys with shadows, some tablelands and quiet waters, and some long stretches of not understanding the journey. But finally, he was home. Looking back, in many ways, we can see that year marked with God's goodness, love, and mercy.

David looks back and realizes that his journey under God's expert care has not always been easy, but God has been there the whole time. He can look back and see goodness, love, and mercy marking his life, and trusts that this will be true until he journeys all the way home and lives with God forever.

This verse also means that God pursues us with goodness, love, and mercy all the days of our lives until we get to heaven where we will live with Him forever. It sounds a lot like the unfailing love, great compassion, and joy of the Good Shepherd in Luke 15.

Whether it's looking back and seeing goodness and love or whether it's knowing God will relentlessly pursue us with goodness and love, both perspectives build our trust in our good and loving God. The kind of shepherding that comes from Him and through Him flows goodness and mercy, points us back to Him, and transforms our days as we look back and see all He has done.

How about you? List three ways you have seen His goodness, love, and mercy in your life.

Lord, thank You that even if we can't see You or how You are working in the moment, we eventually can look back and see Your goodness, love, and mercy. In those places where we can't see it yet, help us to hold on to You, Good Shepherd. Thank You that You promise to pursue us all the days of our lives. O Shepherd, we look forward to the day when we will follow You all the way home. In the journey, You are worthy of our trust. In Jesus' Name, Amen.

DAY 19 - FORGIVEN

Every spring, before I stash it away for the warmer months, I wash our king-size down comforter. The first year I did, I learned a lesson. I crammed my huge, fairly inflexible down comforter into my normal-sized washer. The machine wobbled and clanged, but it worked. It got my down comforter mostly clean, but I am certain I broke my washing machine. Some spring went missing and now it hums and grinds in this weird way, mocking me for my ridiculous belief it could ever handle a king-size load.

I wonder if you, like me, felt you had a king-size load of wash and you looked at God's method of washing, wondering if you could really be clean. I believe we genuinely don't want to dishonor, distrust, or disregard the cross. That's where Jesus washed us clean. But somewhere, deep down inside, we wonder if we have brought to God a load of sin that was just too big to ever really be clean.

I have talked to many people who believe Jesus saved them, even washed them, but still feel stained all the same. They don't "feel" forgiven. Why? One huge reason is Satan tries to keep us emotionally chained to our old story or past, even though spiritually we've been released.

The chains rattle with lies like this: "God will forgive, but that was just. so. much. So, you have to understand you'll be less than others. You'll just have to settle for the fact that this is what you are because of your wandering, dirt, and stains. And you'll never get a life where this doesn't mark you, because you'll always know this is what you did."

I could give voice to so many more lies that many of us have heard after we've confessed and repented of our sins, or I can show you what the voice of God says about being washed.

"Come now, let us reason together," says the LORD. "Though your sins are like scarlet, they shall be white as snow; Though they are red as crimson, they shall be like wool." (Isaiah 1:18)

God calls us to use our *heads* with Him and think this through. Red stains do not come out. Our sin is like that. It is scarlet, red as crimson. Through and through, those sins have dyed our lives permanently.

But God's promise in these verses is that He washes in a way where *red goes to white, white as snow, like wool.* Not a spot of sin left. Your whole load of wash will be white.

You don't have to *feel* like it's white because reality, *reasoning*, truth says it is white. White shows stains. Even the tiniest dot of dirt or speck of red is glaringly obvious. Whiter than snow means there is no sin dirt or sin stain left. If your whole life garment was scarlet, God can take care of it. We can't exhaust His washing or out-dirty His grace. His method of washing can handle the biggest load of crimson, and never break. That's a promise.

Feelings follow thinking, so think with God about the truth that your sins are forgiven, His forgiveness washed away what you were and where you were, and the Good Shepherd has carried you back home into a new life.

God, thank You that the red blood of Jesus and the darkness of His death cleansed all my guilt and stains away. Thank You that He rose again so that I could have a new life and be freed from shame and an old story. I trust You and Your word that when I don't feel forgiven for sins I have already confessed to You I can recite the truth that I am forgiven and bring any feelings under Your banner of Gospel truth. In Jesus' Name, Amen.

DAY 20 - SPOTLIGHT

Then I heard a loud voice in heaven say: "Now have come the salvation and the power and the kingdom of our God, and the authority of his Messiah. For the accuser of our brothers and sisters, who accuses them before our God day and night, has been hurled down. They triumphed over him by the blood of the Lamb and by the word of their testimony...(Rev. 12:10-11b)

And when he finds it, he joyfully puts it on his shoulders and goes home. Then he calls his friends and neighbors together and says, 'Rejoice with me; I have found my lost sheep.'" (Luke 15:5-7)

Our stories as sheep are not about our sin, shame, or wandering. They are about the Shepherd. Stories that celebrate the Shepherd matter to all of us. Therefore, we are called to testify. We are called to give testimony. It's **how** we do it that brings power. What we highlight can be the difference between showcasing sin and dwelling on the past, or being overcomers.

Read Revelation 12:10-11b.
What have now come?

The accuser is Satan. What did he do?

And how did the brothers and sisters overcome him?

Celebrate this deep truth with me in our own stories in Christ. We were accused. Did you feel it? I did. The never-ending shame story, the dragging me to the bottom of the pit covered in sin mess and then accusing me for being so sinful as to be there and accusing me for not being clean enough for God to want to save me. Those are just two! Lies and accusations day and night. The enemy even went to God to spew his hatred for me and argue to have me condemned. He wanted me killed and destroyed. But through the blood of the Lamb salvation came, power in our lives came. That's rescue and healing. He's brought us back! Now, the Kingdom of our God is where we will do our living, and Christ is over all, in us and around us. Our enemy? He has been hurled down.

Verse 11 then tells us we overcame the accuser by the gospel and by the "spoken-Jesus-power" of our testimony. "Word" in the Greek here is "logos." The Gospel of John opens with the unveiling of who Jesus is. John 1:1 tells us, "In the beginning was the Word, and the Word was with God, and the Word was God." Word is logos. Jesus.

We overcome the accusations, the story of our wandering, and the accuser because we are covered by the blood of Jesus and because we speak about what He has powerfully done in our lives. We overcome the enemy by the Jesus of our testimony.

The detrimental opposite is to simply talk about our sin and past. We can give Jesus a role in how we got to where we are today, but that lacks power. It doesn't point to the fact that "now have come salvation and the power and the Kingdom of our God." It points to us, to others, to sin, to messy details, to the past. What we have to tell is Jesus.

Our story, whichever it is—the rescued story, the desire story, the Psalm 23 story, the story yesterday, the story today, the story of hope for tomorrow, the story of that one time when—can only be told in light of Jesus. Spotlight, center stage, the whole stage! Jesus pursued and rescued us. Jesus knew us, was there when we wandered and sinned, became sin for us, and washed our sin away. Jesus was, is, and is to come. Jesus' story is our story.

Jesus is *the story.*

My story about my wandering, my sin, my shame, and my way back is certainly about a life that's changed, but it is not life-changing. His story, Logos, now *that* has power. Through the Logos of our story, He will take sinners and make them overcomers, just like us. That kind of story builds up the faith of others. And we need to tell those stories. Brothers and sisters need to know they are not alone, Who Jesus is, and that what Jesus did for us He can do for them.

Who has told you a personal story or testimony where Jesus got the spotlight? How did that impact your faith?

Part of life in Christ will be gloriously overcoming again and again. It will be telling a story, many stories, stories the world and the Church need to hear. How will you tell *His* story? Think about who Jesus is and what Jesus did. People know about sin and wandering because we all do it. What they need to hear is a focus on Jesus. Highlight three ways that Jesus has shown who He is or what He can do in your life.

Jesus, I am so thankful for Your story: how You pursued me, loved me, carried me home, and changed me. Your story is worth telling. Show me who needs to hear it, and how to focus on You. In Jesus' Name, Amen.

DAY 21 – DRAW NEAR TO GOD

The LORD is near to all who call on Him, to all who call on Him in truth. He fulfills the desires of those who come to Him in [awe and with deep respect]; He hears their cry and saves them. (Psalm 145:18-19)

Let us then approach God's throne of grace with confidence, so that we may receive mercy and find grace to help us in our time of need.
(Hebrews 4:16)

Strong relationships are built on authentic communication. When we are open, honest, honoring, and real then we can truly know each other, trust each other, and support each other. That's an earthly picture of an infinitely greater heavenly reality in our relationship with God.

God wants us to come to Him. He wants us to pursue Him and to be near Him. He loves us so much! He is ready and waiting to hear us talk to Him. He has mercy and grace when we are struggling with temptations and with life in general. He wants to fulfill or reframe our desires with His righteous satisfaction. But we must come to Him.

When we come to Him, we come in three ways:

- **Through Jesus.** It is because of Jesus' death and resurrection that we can draw near to God. There used to be a separation that was symbolized in the Temple by a thick curtain. We could not go near God or have a personal relationship with Him because of His glorious holiness and our sin. But He has forgiven us and made us new, and so the way is open to come to God (Heb. 10:19-22).

- **With humility, respect, and confidence.** We come humbly and with respect, recognizing He is God and we come with confidence that we are His children. We trust His goodness and that His mercy and grace will be the tone and pathway for addressing our struggles and needs.

- **With honesty.** He does not want us to polish things. And we cannot hide our true needs, desires, or motives. He already knows. What He wants is honesty. Read the psalms. They get *really* honest. God isn't shocked by our honesty. In fact, it's when we call on Him and are authentic that He is near to us. Finally, it's not just honesty on our part, but recalling the truth about Who He is and what He can do. That roots us in trust that He can be that or do that again for this situation, need, or desire.

Call out to Him in truth. He is near to you. Come before Him as His child and write your honest, honoring, and confident prayer here.

DAY 22 -MUNDANE QUIET TIME

You may be catching on that part of pursuing Jesus is being in His word. It's when we are in God's word we start to see who He is, what He can do, and who He says we are. It's there that we learn the truth about how Jesus answers our desires or meets our needs, and what it means to follow Him.

Many of us have gone through times when spending time in God's word is somewhat mundane and boring, or it doesn't feel like it's changing our lives. It's dry.

Let's be encouraged by some truths that may help draw us to His word.

It's about learning the "with God" kind of life. Richard Foster reveals that when we approach scripture for information or to "find some formula to solve the pressing need of the moment" our "souls are left untouched." He encourages us to lay down our expectations of what we can get out of it, and come instead with a desire to see what "life with God" looks like, feels like, and what it means. It's from that posture that we start to "learn greater love...All of our study of God's word is so that we might live more and know more of love."

It's a daily. Every morning, I get up and eat one of three things for breakfast. I don't get disappointed that breakfast is breakfast. In fact, I have chosen those three things in particular because they really set me up for a good day. Sometimes it's a fabulous brunch somewhere, and sometimes it's French toast with raspberries. And I love those too. But daily, I know what I need to eat to be well and function well. Similarly, God's word sustains our lives. Sometimes it's wild, amazing, rich, astonishing. And sometimes it's like Tuesday's breakfast--a solid part of our day that we know we will not do well without. And there's a reason for this. Keep reading.

Today's word is tomorrow's victory. The Bible often compares God's word to seed. When it's planted in hearts that are truly open to receiving and responding to it, it takes root and grows. Later there is a huge harvest. I cannot tell you how many times I read a verse one day and a week or even a month later that truth was exactly what I needed. Or how often God taught me small things over time that strung together like pearls until it was a series of interconnected truths that are priceless to me and that I now live by. Like a good breakfast or daily exercise, little by little we see true health. Being in God's word today may be the very thing that He uses for you or through you tomorrow.

We don't know what God's word can do in our lives.
Read Psalm 19:7-11 and see the promises of what His word can do. Circle which one encourages you the most.
The law of the Lord is perfect, refreshing the soul. / The statutes of the Lord are trustworthy, making wise the simple. / The precepts of the Lord are right, giving joy to the heart. / The commands of the Lord are radiant, giving light to the eyes. / The fear of the Lord is pure, enduring forever. / The decrees of the Lord are sure and all of them are righteous. / They are more precious than gold, than much pure gold; / they are sweeter than honey, than honey from the honeycomb. / By them your servant is warned; in keeping them there is great reward.

We may need help. While God's word promises to do all that (and more!), we may need help understanding it. I recommend the YouVersion Bible app. It has a daily verse, a video devo with great insight, and a guided prayer that allows you to move at your own pace in coming before God. Or, grab a great study Bible in an easy-to-read translation like the New Living Translation. The Bible is so rich! We could all use help in understanding it.

We need to SOAR. We may just need a way to engage God's word versus just reading it. Remember, listening and responding always go hand in hand for followers of Jesus. Take one or two verses or a story. Then SOAR. You'll get to experience this tomorrow.:
S - *Stop and pray and then read the scripture.*
O - *Observe what it says.*
A - *Apply.*
R - *Respond.*

Daily walking closely with Jesus means listening and responding to His word. He's calling you and inviting you to come know Him and His love more. He wants to plant seeds in your life that will grow into a harvest. Will you respond?

DAY 23 – TRY IT!

Yesterday we talked about SOAR. Today, we get to try it. If you glance down and the verse is familiar to you, remember that God is here, even in a precious or very familiar verse.

S – Stop and pray and then read the scripture slowly. God's word is alive and active. He will teach you. Ask Him to open your eyes to His word that you might find wondrous things (Ps. 119:18). Then read the passage slowly.

Search me, God, and know my heart;
test me and know my anxious thoughts.
See if there is any offensive way in me,
and lead me in the way everlasting. (Psalm 139:23-24)

O – Observe what it says. *What are the facts? What does it say?*

A – Apply. *Were you struck by anything? What are the lessons? "Is there an example to follow? Warning to heed? Promise to claim? Command to obey?"*[vi]

R – Respond. *What do the facts and application mean to you? Ask God to show you what He is saying to you from this verse or passage.*

Coming to God's word is coming to Him. You aren't interacting with a book. You are creating space for Him to fill, speak, and just be with you.

Use what you experienced and learned in the apply and respond segments of SOAR as a starting point for your prayer today. Commit those to Him.

DAY 24 - LISTENING

But Jesus replied, "It is written and forever remains written, 'Man shall not live by bread alone, but by every word that comes out of the mouth of God.'" (Matthew 4:4, AMP)

My sheep listen to My voice; I know them, and they follow Me.
(John 10:27)

For a year my family lived in another country and our little apartment was in an urban high-rise. There were all kinds of street noises at night: motorcycles zooming, cars revving, bass thumping, people coming out of restaurants, car doors shutting, trash being thrown in dumpsters. When we returned to the U.S., we stayed in a little home surrounded by acres of pasture. At night...

Silence.

So much so that I struggled to sleep for the first few weeks.

Have you noticed how noisy our lives are? Alerts, notifications, social media, news, shows, texts, apps, games, music, traffic, and more. I won't hate on those things. They are in my life too. But I have also noticed that many voices in the world are aiming to capture our attention and keep it. There is a war for our attention, and ultimately for our affection. Who is winning?

Which voice is the loudest in your life?

Who do you really listen to? Who fills your thoughts and mind? What do you rely on for comfort, decisions, and hope?

Jesus wants to be the voice that hushes all the other things that demand your attention. He wants the world to fade while you turn up the volume on His voice. We know His voice through His word and time worshipping and connecting with Him. That voice is the One that wants to give you comfort, guide you, teach you, and give you hope.

When Satan tempted Jesus, he tempted Jesus to meet His own needs apart from God. He was Jesus after all. He could create bread out of stones and feed Himself. And Jesus was hungry. But He would not meet a legitimate need in an illegitimate way. He wouldn't use His power or succumb to the pressure to prove Who He really was to satisfy Himself. God had taken Him there to fast. And so He would take His desire internally and His actual hunger to God. He knew life was more than bread or shortcuts or proving His identity. All that rested in God. Instead, He would look again and again to God's word to meet His real desires and trust that at just the right time, God would righteously meet all His needs. He would listen for God's voice over Satan's and over His own desires and needs.

As the Good Shepherd, He says that we know His voice and follow it. If our lives are too noisy and our attention is scattered, we struggle to hear Him.

Make a choice to turn down or even turn off the voices of the world, and listen for His voice. He has something to say while you want and while you wait. That word will be what sustains you through desires and wants and needs until at just the right time, He meets them legitimately and righteously.

What is some of the noise in your life? What would it look like to turn it down or off and listen to Jesus?

Thank You, Lord, that You speak. Thank You for suffering under the temptation to meet Your own desires, so I could have a sinless Savior Who understands and Who showed me to listen for the One Who can meet my needs and Who holds my identity. I will listen to You, Good Shepherd, and follow You. In Jesus' Name, Amen.

DAY 25 - PRAYER

Ask and keep on asking and it will be given to you; seek and keep on seeking and you will find; knock and keep on knocking and the door will be opened to you. For everyone who keeps on asking receives, and he who keeps on seeking finds, and to him who keeps on knocking, it will be opened. (Matthew 7:7-8, AMP)

This verse is about pursuing God in prayer. It's about coming to Him again and again. He wants us to talk to Him. Just after this Jesus says that hearing our prayers and answering them is like a really good father who wants to care for his children and give them what is good and advantageous to them (v. 11). He wants His children to come and ask, pursue Him, and knock on His door. He'll answer.

"Prayer is not only a personal expression of faith but also a divine invitation from the Lord Himself. Throughout scripture, we are reminded of God's call to pray and seek His presence. The Lord invites us to come before Him with our joys, concerns, and desires, knowing that He hears and responds to the cries of His children. Prayer allows us to connect with the Almighty, align our hearts with His will, and experience His love and guidance in our lives. It is through prayer that we acknowledge our dependence on God, surrender our burdens, and experience the transformative power of His grace. The Lord calls us to prayer, not as a mere duty, but as a means to deepen our relationship with Him, find solace in His presence, and participate in His plans for our lives and the world around us." -- Rachel Saucedo

Have you kept on asking? Are you pursuing Him? Are you knocking on His door? Use the space below to talk and listen to God. Tell Him what you need or want or desire. Draw close to Him. Don't give up. He hears us when we pray (Jer. 29:12-13).

DAY 26 – SEEK HIS FACE

When You said, "Seek My face [in prayer, require My presence as your greatest need]," my heart said to You,
"Your face, O Lord, I will seek [on the authority of Your word]." (Psalm 27:8, AMP)

Here God extends an invitation for us to pursue, or seek Him. The invitation is to seek Him for Himself. It's an invitation to know Him, not just get things from Him. He is the Giver of every good and perfect gift, for sure! We have shared so much about bringing our needs and wants to Him. That's good and set us on His path of righteousness.

In the same breath, many of us know what it means to be wanted for what we can do or give, and not truly known for simply who we are. When our value is only in what we can do, people miss out on the greater gift of knowing us fully. What we can do and offer is a part of that, but that treasure often flows to people who love us for us.

That's the principle here. Surely God wants to meet our needs and answer our prayers. And He wants us to truly know Him. Once we start to seek His face and know Him, we realize He is greater than any "thing" He could give us.

Many are asking, "Who can show us any good?" Let the light of Your face shine upon us, O LORD. You have filled my heart with greater joy and gladness, more than when their new grain and new wine abound.
(Ps. 4:6-7)

When the world is looking for something to satisfy, the truth is having the light of His face—knowing Who He is, His love, His ways, and what truly matters to Him—shine on our lives exceeds what we could imagine as "good" in this life and creates full joy and gladness. More than any new thing people could love or get excited about, His face is what truly satisfies.

I honestly think this takes trying. In Psalm 131, God's word talks about how it's natural for a mother to meet a baby's needs. But there comes a time when the relationship changes. Babies start to be spoon-fed and are weaned from their moms. Mothers are still need-meeters, but the scope of need-meeting starts to broaden. Babies can snuggle and be held without expecting to eat. They become satisfied and settled with a new kind of affection and attention that goes beyond basic needs.

So it is for us spiritually. God is always there to meet our needs. And there's a time when we grow up in our relationship with Him, and start to know Him for more than what He can give. Our souls become still and quiet and satisfied with His presence. We have to grow there. And the way we do is to seek His face—seeking to know Who He is, His love, His ways, and what truly matters to Him.

Take a minute a write down a few things you know about Who He is, His love, His ways, and what truly matters to Him. Sit with Him and focus on those things.

I hear Your invitation to seek Your face and know that You more than anything else are my greatest need and meet my greatest needs. My heart says to You, "I will seek Your face." Let me know You, Your love, Your ways, and what truly matters to You. Let my soul become still and quiet and satisfied with Your presence. In Jesus' Name, Amen.

DAY 27 – YOU ARE NOT ALONE

"Those who know Your name trust in You, for You, LORD, have never forsaken those who seek You." (Psalm 9:10)

"Tears began to flow down my face as I immersed myself in worship during a Sunday morning church service a few weeks ago. As I raised my voice in praise, I fully surrendered all my fear and anxiety about all the changes taking place in my home, and I entered into the presence of the Lord. The presence of the Lord is a place I long to be. There is no fear, no anxiety, and no challenges in the presence of God. Just peace that passes all understand and a gracious Savior that invites us to rest in Him. As I continued to worship, I heard Him whisper to my heart, "I have not forsaken you." More tears and praises washed over me. I soon realized how reassuring and calming the words, "I have not forsaken you," are to a weary soul. A sweet, simple whisper of a phrase to my heart, provided much-needed comfort on that Sunday morning and throughout the weeks to come.

Within the past two weeks, my youngest daughter started high school in a new education model, my oldest daughter started college, and my husband starts a new job on Monday. There are big changes happening in our home and while many of these are positive events, they come with a variety of emotions for everyone to process.

I do not know where you are today. You might, like me, be in a season of rapid change, or maybe you are in a season of stability. I know that many of us fight battles that others do not see. But our loving Heavenly Father sees, and I am here to remind you today that He has not forsaken you. He is right there with you. Continue to seek after Him and invite His presence into your life and you will find never-ending comfort and peace." – Misty Henry

To know His name is to understand, declare, proclaim, and confess Who God is and what He can do. To know His name increases our faith and encourages us. That means we literally can take courage from Him and have it infused into our hearts.

Take a moment and talk to God out loud about Who He is and what He can do. If you need help, try using Psalm 86:15 as a starting point.: *But You, O LORD (the One Who chooses me, loves me, redeems me, and keeps His promises), are a compassionate and gracious God, slow to anger, abounding in love and faithfulness.*

Thank You, God, that You never, never, no not ever, never leave us or forsake us (Heb. 13:5[vii]). If you say something twice in Your word, it's important. Three times is critical. Five times? You really mean You will never leave or forsake me. I know Your name and I am still learning. Help me to trust in You and take courage from You. In Jesus' Name, Amen.

DAY 28 – FINDING OUR TRUE DESIRES

Trust in the LORD and do good; dwell in the land and enjoy safe pasture. Delight yourself in the LORD and He will give you the desires of your heart. (Psalm 37:4)

This verse is quoted pretty often and is a favorite for many. I love it too! Here God is communicating how He takes our desires and reframes them to truly identify what we want or need so that He can meet them or exceed them.

When it comes to understanding our true desires, it starts with trust. We must trust God: trust His goodness, His plan, His nearness, and His love. When we trust Him, we stay close to Him and follow Him. That's the "do good, dwell in the land, and enjoy safe pasture." Sounds a lot like our journey through Psalm 23.

With trust, as we pursue Him we enjoy His nearness, presence, and provision, and take joy in following Him. We know Who He is, His love, His ways, and what truly matters to Him. That's delight! So when we bring our desires to God, in the framework of trust, joyfully following, and knowing Him, one of two things happens:

He meets our desires and needs by giving or providing something, or He reframes our desires.

Sometimes, it may be that we don't understand what we truly want. We've practiced this. We go to God and say, "I am thinking and feeling that if I only had _____ I'd be/feel _____. What do I feel like I really need or desire here?" He will reveal what's going on inside if we ask. So if I felt like I would be truly valued if this person paid attention to me, and I brought that to God, He would remind me that my value is not in who sees or acknowledges me, because they are just people. My value rests in the truth that I belong to Him and His eyes are on me all day long. He sees and knows who I am and what I do, and He loves me.

Sometimes it's that we want a good thing, even a right thing, and God has something different. Jonah wanted God to strike down a whole city of his enemies who were godless and some of the most violent people on earth. He was so mad when God gave them a message of repenting and then didn't turn the city to ash. Jonah even said he knew Who God was and His ways, but he still wanted justice. Wanting justice is a good thing. In this case, God chose mercy. He reframed Jonah's desire with God's greater desire and plan. Jonah didn't like it, but God was still merciful to a city that repented.

Or take Joseph. When Mary told him she was pregnant, Joseph had every right by the law to divorce her. He desired to quietly do the right thing. God intervened and reframed Joseph's desire by showing him the bigger plan of Jesus and salvation. Joseph took the new desire God was giving—the new plan, the greater gift, the better path.

In both stories, to get God's best, they had to set aside their own desire so they could want God and God's way instead. This is not easy, and especially for Joseph, life would prove hard. But God was literally with him and he would play one of the most important roles in history—being the loving earthly father who provided for and protected Jesus while He grew up.

When God reframes our desires, we lay aside the original question about what we want and we start asking, "Am I wanting God?" When we want God, then we delight in Him and He will place in our hearts new desires or deep satisfaction in Him or resolute faith to trust His goodness and ways for us as He provides something different.

Again, it's not easy, but He is good. We can trust Him that He has our best at heart, and will give that to us at just the right time.

Think about a time when God has reframed or replaced a desire of your heart. How did you come to know Him better because of His best for you?

Thank You, God, that You are good. I trust You to put in me the desires of my heart, knowing You will meet them. In Jesus' Name, Amen.

DAY 29 – GENTLE WITH THOSE WHO STRUGGLE

Brothers, if anyone is caught in any sin, you who are spiritual [that is, you who are responsive to the guidance of the Spirit] are to restore such a person in a spirit of gentleness [not with a sense of superiority or self-righteousness], keeping a watchful eye on yourself, so that you are not tempted as well. (Galatians 6:1, AMP)

We who are strong must be considerate of those who are sensitive about things like this. We must not just please ourselves. We should help others do what is right and build them up in the Lord.
(Romans 15:1-2)

If we are God's sheep, we are all in this together! Isaiah 53 tells us that each one of us has gone astray and gone our way and ultimately Jesus had to pay for our sin by His brutal death on the cross.

As we follow Jesus, we will see other sheep wander and follow their noses. We will see sheep come back with the Shepherd. Those sheep may be us!

If we're all sheep, then let us take the heart of Jesus and be humble and gentle towards one another. There are a few ways we can do this.

First, when we are in close community with each other, we commit to caring for each other and calling each other up into true life in Christ. This means we will graciously and gently listen and talk to one another about what it looks like for Christ to be in our lives, including in our struggles and stumbling. For example, I was with my best friend lamenting a situation I was in and sharing all the heavy details with her. She listened, but as a godly friend, she sensed I was being pulled away by my pride and by a complaining attitude. When I was done, she looked at me and said, "You know what, Gin? It's not about you." Ouch. But so true. She wasn't mean, and she wasn't trying to be God or speak for Him. She was just truthful and clear because she knew and loved me. And like a door opening on a dark room, I could see the situation clearly, including my sin, and we talked about Christ's way for me in this situation.

The other thing that could have happened is she could have piggy-backed on that and poured out her complaints and pride on a similar situation, and like sheep, we could have gorged on this all the way beyond the root to the yuck underneath and both been cast down. She could have been tempted but chose to point me back to Jesus instead. How faithful.

Second, we need to be patient with sheep who come back. They may still bear the marks of their wandering and they may have fresh sensitivities to things to stay close to the Shepherd. They may not be able to do, go, watch, see, or listen to some things that we can. Instead of judging or getting irritated that they have less freedom than us, let's encourage them in their fresh walk with Jesus and celebrate them following Him. "They" may someday be us. And wouldn't we want grace and kindness and encouragement?

Finally, rejoice with the Shepherd. Come to the celebration and rejoice over His heart of compassion, love, and grace.

Can you think of anyone who has recently started following Jesus or come back to Jesus? How can you be gentle, humble, patient, kind, true, and encouraging to them?

Next, if you don't have close friends who follow Jesus and speak the truth in love to you, where can you find those? How can you be that friend for someone else?

Lord, I am one of the sheep that went astray. You died for me. May I always remember I belong to a flock of redeemed sheep covered by Your grace. May Your gentleness, grace, truth, and encouragement flow from me, and may I humbly receive faithful words from godly friends when they sense I might wander. Calling one another up into life in Christ is not judgment but gentle faithfulness. Help me to be that kind of friend too. In Jesus' Name, Amen.

DAY 30 – FURTHER PURSUING JESUS

Insert *I have loved you, My people, with an everlasting love. With unfailing love I have drawn you to Myself.* (Jeremiah 31:3)

As the Father has loved Me, so have I loved you. Now remain in My love. (John 15:9)

How wide, long, high, and deep do you think God's love is for Jesus? Describe how much God loves His Son, Jesus.

That is how Jesus loves you.

You didn't earn it or deserve it. But He loves you with that kind of love. And He wants your whole life to be soaked in knowing that love.

We don't pursue God to be loved by Him. We are loved by Him and so we pursue (follow) Him. We can't do anything to make Him love us more. We can't do anything to make Him love us less. It's not in our doing, it's in His done on the cross that brings us into a love relationship with Him where we can live in His love.

When I think about a love relationship with Jesus, I think about the best, most loving relationships in my life. Those are with my husband, best friend, and sister. How about you? Who are the people that you have the best, most loving relationships with?

The best relationships have planned and spontaneous connections. They talk, share, and listen. They hang out and do fun things together that they both enjoy. They encourage each other and focus on each other's best. The best relationships take time, and time takes sacrifice. The same is true in further pursuing Jesus. We have already explored how to daily connect with Him in things like talking to Him, listening to Him through prayer and His word, taking our needs and wants to Him, gratitude, wonder, and resting with Him. Let those times be both planned and spontaneous.

To pursue Him further…

Take time to cultivate things you love together. What do you love about God? How can you focus on that? Where do you go to see that on display? What is God's heart for? How and where can you be a part of that? Answer that here.

Serve Him. "The word 'ministry' comes from a Latin term meaning 'one who has to do with small things'." The backdrop of the word ministry is "humility and service." For us, that includes God's call to serve Him and love others. We can't do it on our own. The Spirit guides and fuels us in serving.[viii] When you know what God's heart is for, join Him there, and serve Him, you will see Him and experience Him as you do it with the strength He provides (1 Pet. 4:11b).

Honor, love, and be aligned with Him. Jesus goes on to say in John 15 that if we love Him we will obey Him. What this means is that as we soak in and live in His love, out of love for Him we will want to follow Him closely and be a part of His best for us. We will want to honor Him in what we think, say, and do. This means we will listen to Him and respond in love. We will obey.

What has pursuing Jesus looked like for you in the last several weeks? What have you experienced?

What does pursuing Him further look like for you? It'll be a lifelong journey, so listen to His Spirit here and take the next small step.

Jesus, thank You for Your vast, almost incomprehensible love for me. I want to soak and live in that love. Show me which step to take next to keep pursuing and following You. In Jesus' Name, Amen.

ABOUT THE AUTHOR

Ginny surrendered her life to Christ when she was twenty. Since that moment it has been her passion to "proclaim His praise and tell of all His wonderful deeds" (Ps. 26:7). Ginny has been called by God to help others know His truth, wholeness, and purpose for their lives. Her passion and calling have played out in ministry by being a wife and mother of two grown children, serving in her church with students and small groups, and being in full-time ministry for over 15 years. She joyfully serves as Chief Spiritual Development Officer for Lionheart Children's Academy and is working on her Master's in Spiritual Formation. When she is not reading or studying, prepping for her small group, or working on her latest project, you can find Ginny walking her dog, booking her next trip, riding on a motorcycle with her husband Chip, or drinking a hot cup of coffee while folding a fresh load of laundry. Honestly, she loves that last thing a lot.

[i] Ryan McCarthy, www.ccbcfamily.org.
[ii] https://www.discovermagazine.com/technology/phone-notifications-are-messing-with-your-brain
[iii] Jeff Vanderstelt
[iv] Smith, James K.A., You Are What You Love: The Spiritual Power of Habit. Grand Rapids: Brazos Press, 2016. 15.
[v] Elisabeth Elliot
[vi] Anne Graham Lotz provides this method in many of her Bible studies.
[vii] In the Greek, there are five negatives in this verse, showing how serious God is about being with us.
[viii] Dr. Mara Lief Crabtree, Regent University

A special acknowledgement to W. Phillip Keller and Zondervan publishers for his book A Shepherd Looks at Psalm 23. This was a significant source for Days 10-18. That book has made a lasting impression on my walk with Christ and on my leadership.

Made in United States
Orlando, FL
07 September 2023